My Journey

By Raymond Bui

COPYRIGHT NOTICE

No part of this publication may be reproduced, distributed, or transmitted in any form or by any means, including photocopying, recording, or other electronics or mechanical methods. without the prior written permission of the publisher, except in the case of brief quotations embodies in crital reviews and certain other noncomercial uses permitted by copyright law.

ISBN: 9780960059140 (Paperback).

LCCN: 2019942156

Published by Clover Leaves Publishing. Illustrated by Hubert Bui.

Printed and bound in United States of America.

Copyright 2019@ by Raymond Bui. All right reserved.

Raymond Bui

SUMMARY

I am a newly Graduate at University of California, Merced, applying for admission into US Medical school and Tier 1 Caribbean school of Medicine.

EDUCATION

UC Merced. BS Human Biology. May 2019

- Biology 1   Molecular Biology
- Cell Biology   CSE 1
- Microbial Evolution   Genetics
- Immunology   Biochemistry
- Organic Chem I   Organic Chem II

TRAINING

- National EMT Certification training July 2018
- American Red Cross   2013-2015
- Job shadow at Seton Medical center   Feb 2019 to Present.

EXTRACURRICULAR ACTIVITIES

- United States Naval Sea Cadet Corps   2010-2015
- Grey Ghost Division, Alameda, CA   Petty Officer 3rd
- Alpha Phi Omega   2016 - Present

SKILLS & CAPABILITIES

- CPR certified (5/31/2018)
- Ambulance Driver License
- HTML Programming Language
- Publish first book: My Journey, June 2019 and sale on Amazon.

Personal Statement

My journey to becoming a physician is to find a home at XXXX University School of Medicine. My name is Raymond Bui, and here is how the journey started.

My mom was a registered vascular technologist; therefore, she was able to teach me about the human body at a very early age. Throughout my elementary school years, my interest in the medical field grew. One television show I began watching was **House**. In that show, a doctor saves people though unorthodox ways. What really caught my interest were the diseases patients contracted and how they were affected. While many diseases that the show highlighted weren't extremely common in today's world, it was still fascinating to see how patients' bodies reacted. I believe that it was around this point when I developed my first reason to become a physician: I wanted to see how diseases affect us and how we can combat them.

I became especially interested in parasitic diseases. There was a show on the Animal Planet network called **Monsters Inside Me**, documentaries about actual people who contracted parasites. I learned how parasites can leach the body of nutrients, causing complications. One episode that disturbed but also fascinated me concerned a brain-eating amoeba that gave amoebic meningitis to an 11-year-old child swimming in a dirty lake. The parasite acts by invading the nervous system and shutting it down. Ultimately, the child succumbed to the disease, which not only scared me, but also motivated me to study in the medical field. I don't want another young kid to die due to a disease that doesn't have a cure yet.

By the time I got into college, I began having doubts about a medical career. Initially, I tried pursuing independent study without seeking help. Unfortunately, that method of studying didn't work out for me because I began struggling in all of my biology courses. I even considered changing my major to something else. For instance, two classes that I severely struggled with at first were Organic Chemistry 1 and Immunology. I couldn't get the full grasp of how structures were formed, so I started seeking tutors for help. At the beginning of these courses, I had D's, which at the time was common for the class, but still demoralizing. By the end of the semester, I had passed the classes with B's. This wouldn't have been possible if I had not been motivated or determined to learn the material as best as I could. Fortunately, after several tutoring sessions, I began taking an interest in Organic Chemistry and Immunology fundamentals. Thankfully, tutors helped me piece together everything about these subjects.

Before the end of the course, I was able to essentially give a lecture on how the entire immune system worked from top to bottom, and my grade jumped because of it. Despite the difficulty of those courses, I had a fun time understanding their concepts. Ultimately, I decided to stick to my path of studying medicine.

Since I had finished all of my required classes early, I took the opportunity during my last semester to prepare for the MCAT and to develop patient care experience. As I was EMT certified, I planned to look for an EMT position. Instead, I found an opportunity to work at Seton Medical Center, located in Daly City, California. I am at the hospital three days a week. OnMondays and Wednesdays, I work in the Radiology department, where techs perform x-rays. I mainly walk around the hospital with a tech and run the film in a machine that makes the x-ray images. Of course, I'm not licensed to take the actual x-ray itself. Usually, most patients I get have fractured bones either in the legs or arms. Sometimes patients come due to other factors, such as shortness of breath or gastrointestinal problems. These patients could either be outpatients or those located in the ER or the ICU. Every Friday I go to the Diagnostic Department. Usually, I get to help and watch a tech use ultrasound to look at a patient's blood vessels to find any abnormalities. Additionally, I am able to look at echo techs using ultrasound to do echocardiograms or doing EKGs for heart rhythm measurements. However, the main reason why I go to this department on Fridays is because occasionally a surgeon, Dr. Millhouse, will come by and perform a diagnosis on a patient. One time, he took me with him to go see a catheter insertion in a patient. I was able to see Dr. Millhouse insert a catheter up close to a patient's compressed artery and expand it somore blood could flow in. I have attended XXXX seminars in San Francisco a few times, due to my interest in your program. Each time I have come away more convinced that your school offers a path with great resources to keep my dream alive. I hope you consider me as a future student for XXXX University Medical School

Index

1. At Birth. — 7
2. In First Grade. — 8
3. Youth In Medicine. — 10
4. Being A Sea Cadet Recruit And Become Petty Officer in 5th Year. — 11
5. High School Graduation. — 16
6. U.C. Merced is Next Place Away from Home.
7. A Semester Off in Prepation for New Beginning.
8. College Graduation in May 18, 2019. — 31

At Birth

As a happy camper, I seemed to be comfortable inside Mom's tummy. The labor lasted more than 10 hour without birth crowning. Finally, Mom got C-section while Dad still read the book "What to expect when you are expecting"

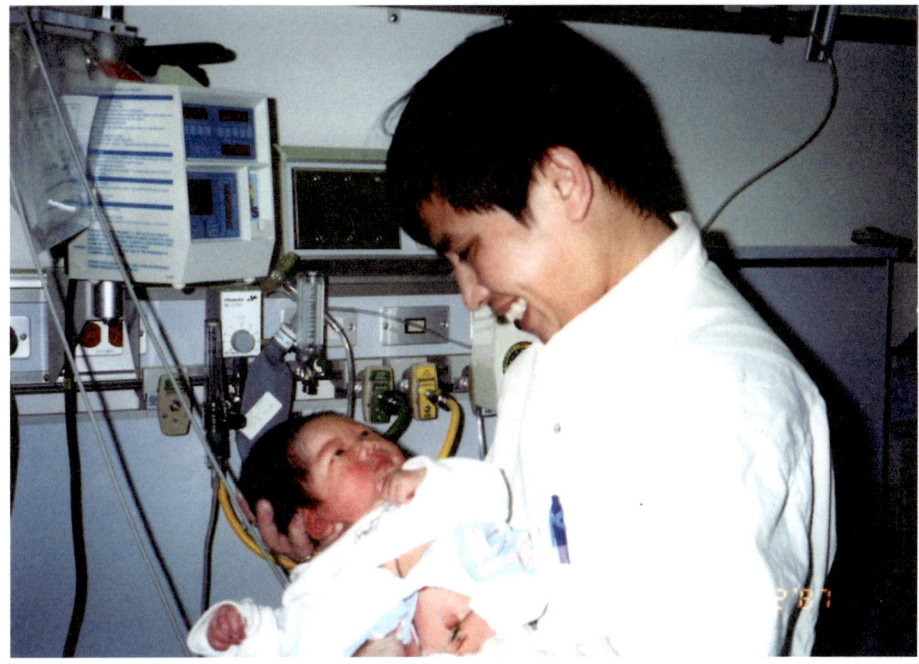

From early years, I was always proud that I looked like Mom. What was a Gene?

My Brother and I, before and after.

In First Grade

I was sharing my dream when I became US President as shown:

Parent's Guide if I were missing:

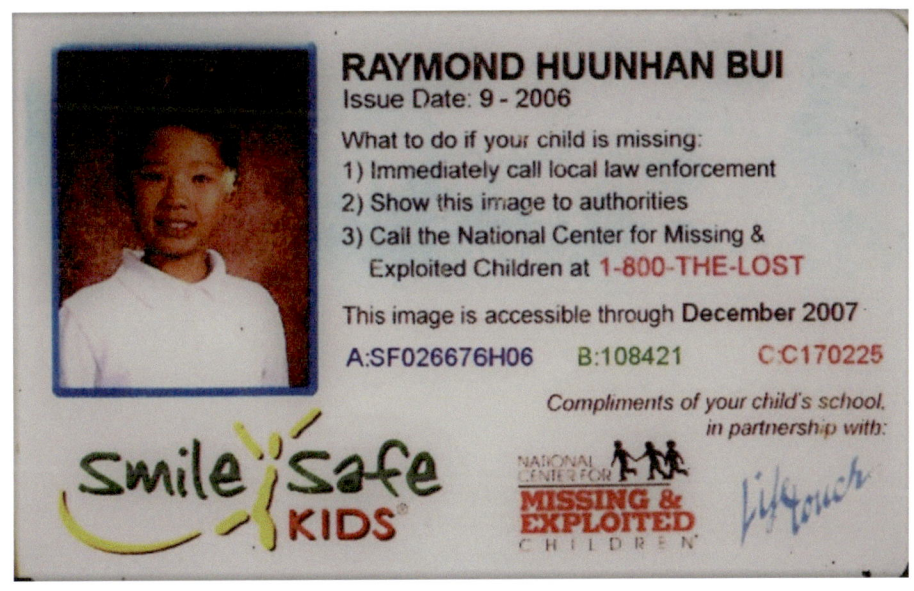

Here was an opportunity to learn medicine when I was young

How To Become A Petty Office From A Recruit In Sea Cadet Program

Sea Cadet Recruit Training
2011
Certificate of Graduation

Presented to U. S. Naval Sea Cadet

RECRUIT RAYMOND BUI, NSCC

In recognition of your successful completion of all requirements of Sea Cadet Recruit Training and thereby has qualified in part to advance in the Naval Sea Cadet Corps. Presented on this Thirtieth Day of July, Two Thousand Eleven at NAS Lemoore, Lemoore, CA

Lcdr Laneya Littrell, NSCC
LCDR Laneya Littrell, USNSCC
COTC, Recruit Training 2011

The 2 week recruit training was very hard. if I could survive this and I can succed in life.

The hard work always counts !!!

UNITED STATES NAVAL SEA CADET CORPS
GREY GHOST DIVISION

Certificate of Award

This is to certify that

E3 RAYMOND BUI, NSCC

Has met all requirements for and is hereby awarded the

FIFTH YEAR SERVICE RIBBON

At USS HORNET CVS-12 PIER 3, ALAMEDA, CA
This Nineteenth Day of September, Two Thousand and Fourteen

Paul Norton
LTjg Paul Norton, NSCC
Commanding Officer

CERTIFICATE
of
COMPLETION

May it be known that

Raymond Bui

ha*s successfully completed*

PETTY OFFICER LEADERSHIP ACADEMY

And is awarded the
NSCC Torch Appurtenance

This Twenty-Second day of June in the year Two Thousand Thirteen
At Coast Guard Island, Alameda, CA

Marcia L. Powell, LCDR, NSCC
Petty Officer Leadership Academy

James Monahan, USN (Ret)
Executive Director

HIGH SCHOOL YEARS WENT WITH FUN AND SOME SADNESS

My Grandfather passed away in 2013. The very first time, I experienced the death of a loved one.

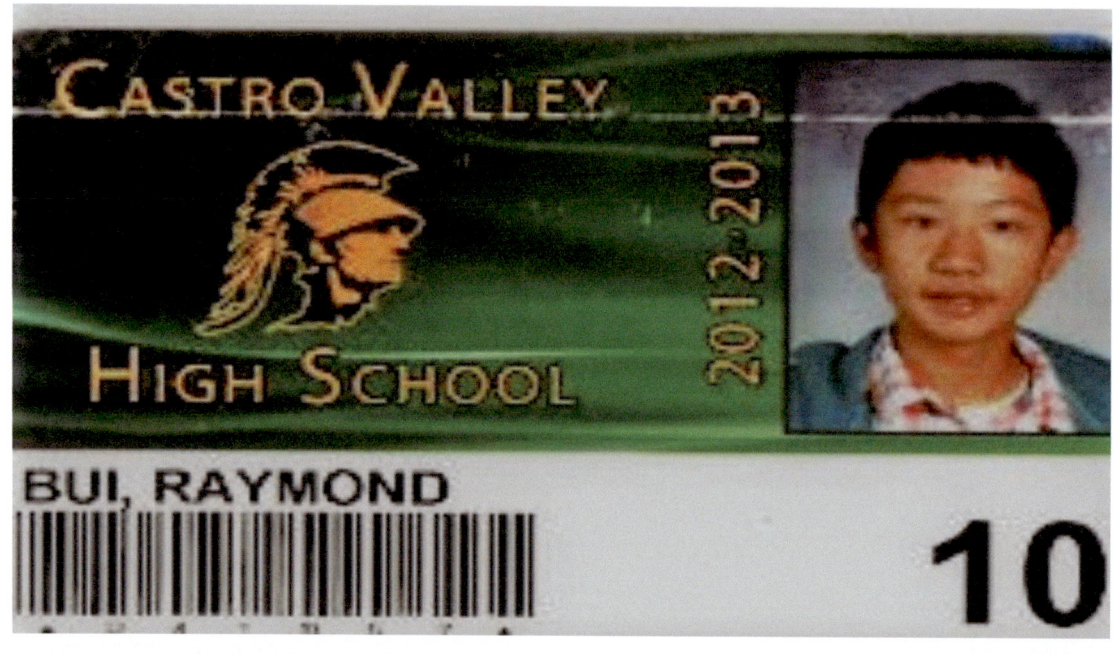

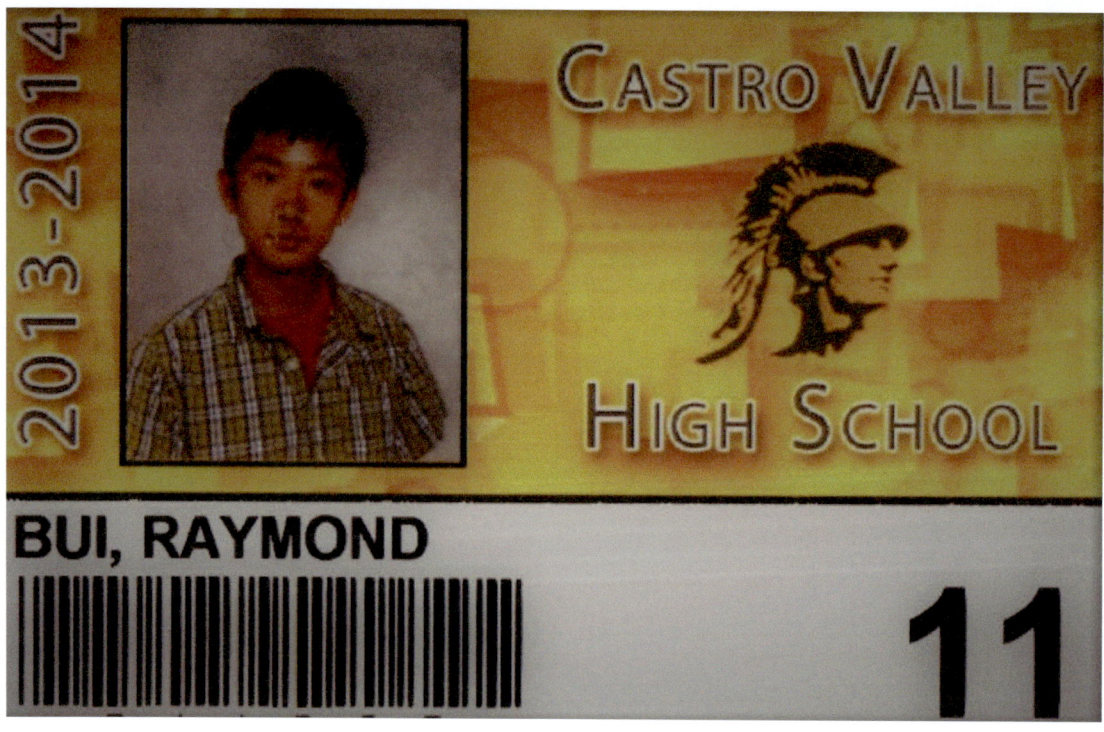

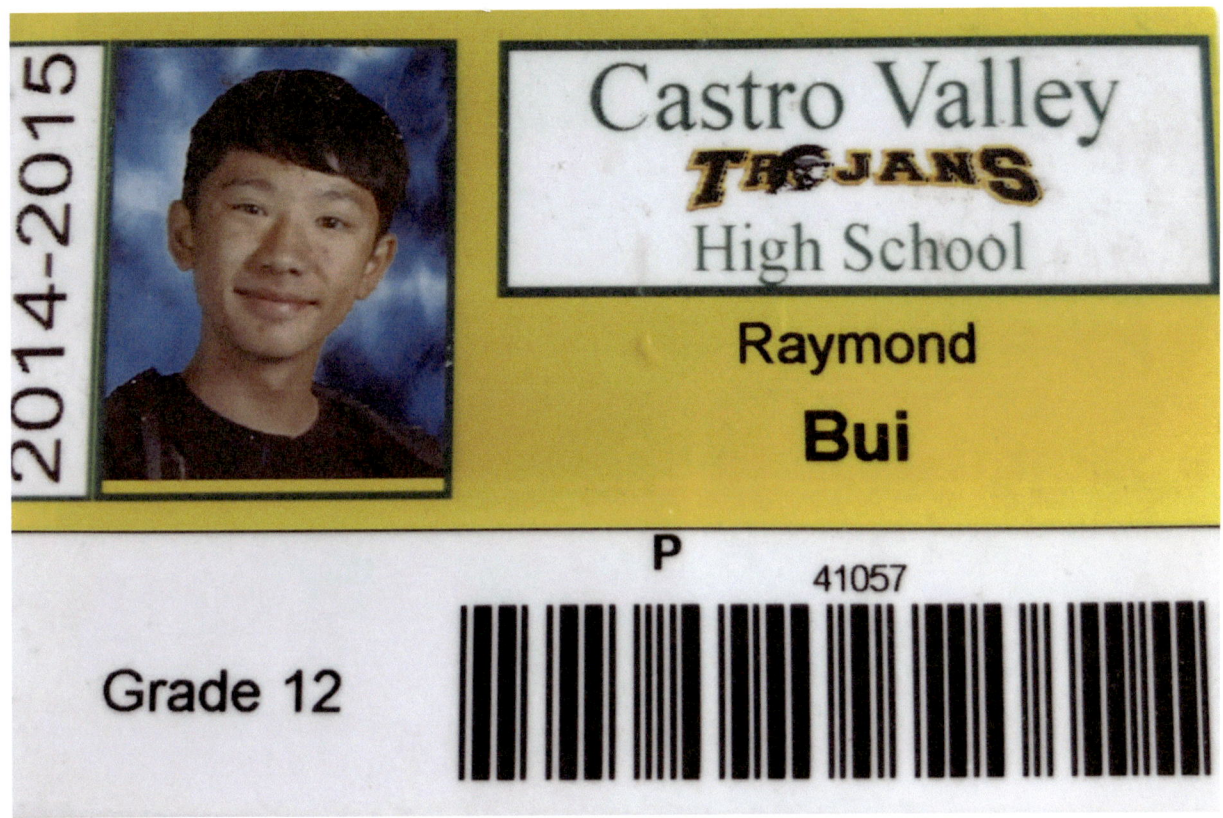

I was ready to leave home for UC Merced while my dad left his 20 years career as an Electrical Engineer to becoming a Cancer Registrar at UC San Francisco. And yet, my younger brother was going to my old school. What was a year!

HIGH SCHOOL GRADUATION CLASS 2015

Castro Valley High School

HIGHEST HONORS (GPA of 4.0 or higher)

Suhani Abdullah, Morgan Adams, Raymond Akagi, Maria Avellan Arditto, Mitch Avery, Merna Aziz, Sophie Baylon, Maria Bellamacina, Katherine Blake, Daniel Den Briones, Brenden Brown, Kyle Chan, Daniel Chen, Joanna Chen, Ryan Chen, YiQi Chen, Angela Chiang, Ernest Chow, Diamond Chu, Nicholas Dang, Dominic Diaz, Eduardo Diaz, Andrew Do, Jia Du, Milana Egorova, Jeffrey Fallejo, William Fong, Andrew Gordeev, Allen Guo, Carmen Hom, Christine Hong, Kiana Hosseinian, Kenneth Huang, Kyman Huang, Stephanie Huerta, Shoyo Inokuchi, Leslie Irwin, Christina Jin, Eleanor Kaj, Kiranpreet Kaur, Micah Kim, Katelyn King, Gordon Kole, Fiona Kong-Dismuke, Amanda Korbas, Clarisa Kusumonegoro, HyeokBin Kweon, Joanna Lam, Aimee Ledbetter, Alvin Lee, Victor Lee, Helen Liao, Brittany Lopes, Patrick Low, Mika Lucas, Bethany Lum, Ian Maloney, Kevin Mao, Juan Mariscal, Yemi Mock, Genaro Morales Lopez, Kevin Morimoto, Collette Moura, Martin Mourgos, Kevin Moyung, Maya Para, Khang Pham, Rose Pica, Devin Pon, Tanisha Potnis, Simran Sahota, Katrina Seto, YeEun Tak, Anna Talajkowski, Brian Truong, Timson Tse, Jeffrey Van, Deric VanDamme, Angela Wong, Haybie Wong, Allison Woo, Marissa Wu, Jessica Xie, Kevan Yang, Willow Yang, Lorcan Yeung, Sarah Yi, Caroline Yu, Peter Zaleski, Joshua Zeitsoff, James Zhen, Sunny Zhou

HIGH HONORS (GPA of 3.75 - 3.99)

Taylor Ajlouny, Samin Akter, Sasha Anguiano, Jake Augustine, Kimberly Barclay, Adam Blum, Jocelyn Bonilla-Araujo, Andrea Chen, Erin Cherniss, Kristi Cheung, Michael Chourappa, Margaux Chow, Andrew Chuong, Dane Clemensen, Katherine Curtin, Stefan Gabriel Dollaga, Katie Farnham, Mitchell Fredrickson, Michael French, Dustin Giang, Alejandro Gonzalez, Marcello Guzman Bejarano, Darren He, Brian Ho, Ada Huang, Yu Chi Huang, Youngwon Hwang, Grey Janowski, Amritnam Kaur, Sarah Keil, Diana Kho, Sarah Kim, Jocelyn Kirley, Rachel Kong, Yuliana Kostyuk, King Law, Vanessa Ledezma, Zoe Leonardo, Elaine Li, HaYoung Lim, Rani Lu, Correll Maley, Nathan Mok, Estephany Moncada, Michaela Nash, Ling Kwan Ng, Miranda Nild, Kaitlyn Ohara, Roger Ou, Alexis Pagan, Emily Patton, Maia Peterson, Cody Phan, Haley Pryde, Spencer Purdy, Paulina Rak, Andrew Raymond, Danielle Rice, Madison Salvato, Michelle Schantz, Deepa Sharma, Yenah Shin, Jesse Singh, Jenna Sparks, Katrina Sponsler, Jonathan Stewart, Andy Tang, Kathryn Truong, Tyler Wang, Vanessa Watson, Jaliya Wilkinson, Sarah Wohlner, Anthony Wong, Priscilla Wong, Michaela Wood, Austin Xing-Le, Michelle Yeung, Annie Yu

HONORS (GPA of 3.50 - 3.74)

Wajiullah Abdullah, Carly Andrade, Emma Armstrong, Christopher Baker, Karess Batkowski, Melisa Bay, Laila Birznieks, Valdis Birznieks, Kendall Bonvicin, Raymond Bui, Daniel Cervantez, Breanna Chaves, Melanie Cheung, Anthony Chew, Javier Corral, Lien Dao, Corban De La Vega, Alison Dhont, Jessica Lauren Domingo, Jasmine Edwards, Kendrick Edwards, Sarah Ehsan, Christopher Fong, Munkhzul Galbadrakh, Daniel Ghoukassi, Nolan Glock, Tailor Goods, Viana Goodwin, Sarah Hahn, Oriana Hale, Sabrina Ham, Marina Hanna, Brandon Holyoake, Joanna Huang, Julie Huang, Michael Huang, Tim Huang, Siobhan Ip, Isabella Jacoby, Lauren Jelks, Morgan Johnson, Lisa Keebler, Cailin Keenan, Ian Kwan, Liam Landy, Ryan Lawrence, Ashlee Leite, Maria Meawad, Dana Moehle, Seth Morrison, Sabrina Murugesu, Jamaica Musca, Chelsea Nash, Laura Navarro, Nicholas Ong, Amelia Ortiz, Seung Park, Saawan Patel, Raquel Polanco, Cheuk Pun, Lior Raskin, Brandon Riddell, Soneeya Sanjel, Francesca Sardina, Kaylyn Sheriff, Kyle Shiluk, Madeline Siem, Shivam Singh, Margarita Sorokina, Derick Truong, Jaywood Tse, Insun Von Euw, Olivia Wallace, Braxton Waxdeck, Amanda Wong, Daniel Wong, Justin Wong, Jasmin Zhang

NATIONAL MERIT FINALIST

Andrew Gordeev
Kenneth Huang
Victor Lee
Willow Yang
Joshua Zeitsoff
James Zhen

Athletic Awards and Scholarships

Boston University	Kennedy Jones
Claremont McKenna College	Brenden Brown
CSU Cal Poly San Luis Obispo	Allison Woo
CSU Chico	Cailin Keenan
CSU East Bay	Aaron Jones, Joseph Dimitratos, Mariah Ford
Dillard University	Stephanie Coates
Holy Names University	Tailor Goods
Northern Arizona University	Carter Mackey
St. Mary's College	Jasmine Edwards
UC Berkeley	Carson Sand, Miranda Nild
UC Davis	Cameron Edwards, Emma Armstrong
UC Santa Cruz	Jenna Sparks
Herculean Award	Emma Armstrong, Dane Clemenson, Carter Mackey, Miranda Nild
Chuck Fehely Memorial Scholarship	Mitch Avery and Blake Brown
CVHS Athletics Boosters	Emma Armstrong, Mitch Avery, Erica Gorman, Mohamed Musa

Being a Pilot, I Can Fly High And Navigate My Journey To

My next home is UC Merced

College Years 2015 -2019 and ....

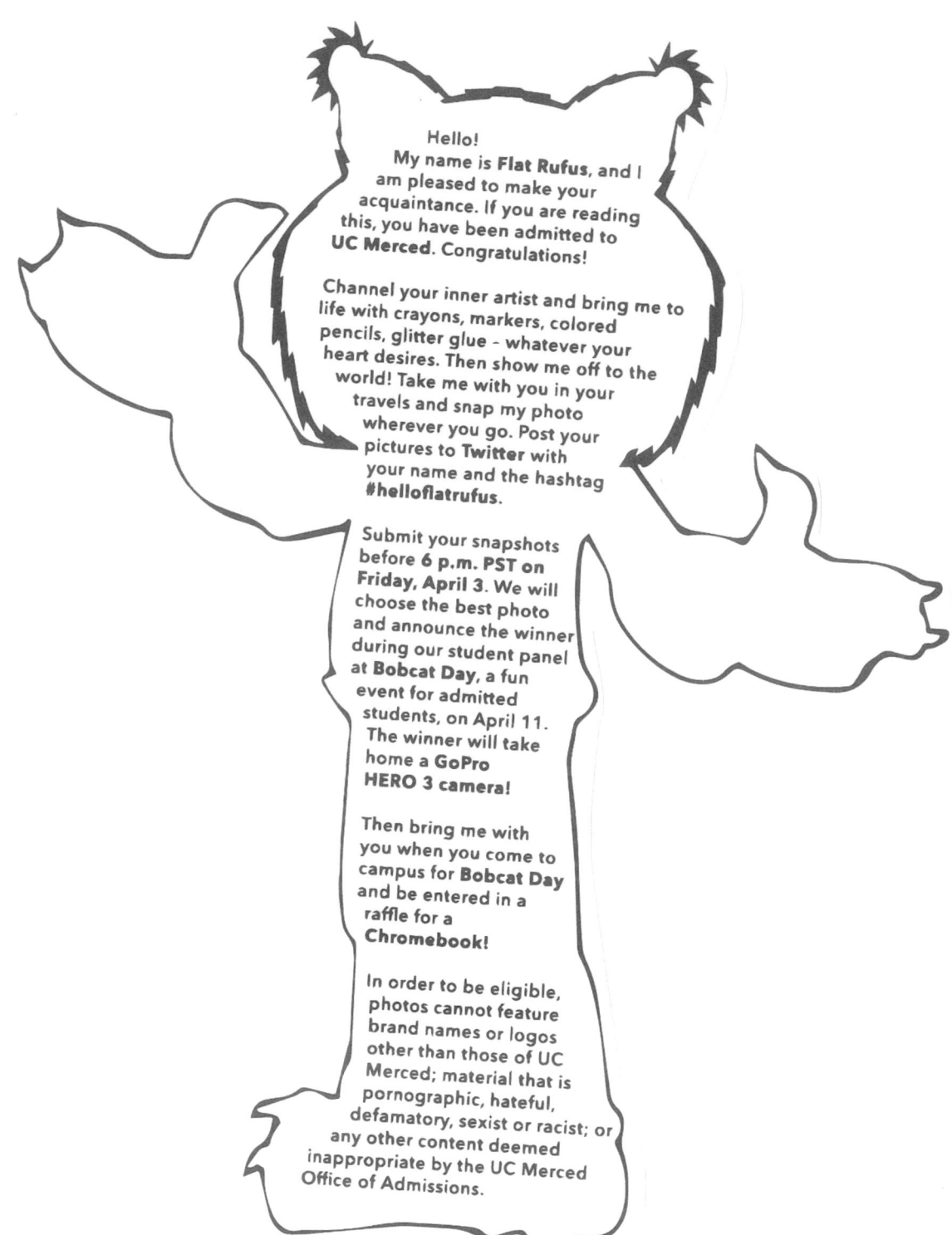

Hello! My name is **Flat Rufus**, and I am pleased to make your acquaintance. If you are reading this, you have been admitted to **UC Merced**. Congratulations!

Channel your inner artist and bring me to life with crayons, markers, colored pencils, glitter glue - whatever your heart desires. Then show me off to the world! Take me with you in your travels and snap my photo wherever you go. Post your pictures to **Twitter** with your name and the hashtag **#helloflatrufus**.

Submit your snapshots before 6 p.m. PST on **Friday, April 3**. We will choose the best photo and announce the winner during our student panel at **Bobcat Day**, a fun event for admitted students, on April 11. The winner will take home a **GoPro HERO 3 camera!**

Then bring me with you when you come to campus for **Bobcat Day** and be entered in a raffle for a **Chromebook!**

In order to be eligible, photos cannot feature brand names or logos other than those of UC Merced; material that is pornographic, hateful, defamatory, sexist or racist; or any other content deemed inappropriate by the UC Merced Office of Admissions.

SUMMER 2018 A New Preparation

- ❖ **EMT Basic Training from May 21 – June 28 with American Health Education.**
- ❖ **JUN 30 Immunotherapy Patient Summit - San Francisco by Cancer Research Institute**

Post conference Abstract

Cancer cells are our essentially our cells with their blueprints changed. It's not like a simple pathogen like bacteria or viruses where our immune cells can easily get rid of. The problem with these cancer cells is that they're technically a normal human cell, but with enough changes that leeches off nutrients from other cells that need them. Since their discovery, several methods of combating Cancer have been discovered, with the most successful one being immunotherapy.

Immunotherapy is editing your immune cells so that they are able to recognize and kill these cancer cells. There's a lot of mechanisms that go behind this, but the best analogy is giving a police officer the right gun to stop the right criminals. There are several different options of immunotherapy. First one is targeting antibodies. The antibodies produced by cancer cells mimic proteins produced by the immune system so normally they would remain undetectable. By having our T cells recognize them, the cancer would no longer live. Another method is the use of immunomodulators which blocks or activates certain cellular pathways that allow our immune system to recognize and kill the cancer cells. Without going too in-depth, there are signal pathways that would be altered so cancer cells could survive and proliferate. Perhaps the most popular method is adoptive cell therapy, or CAR T. Scientists extract our T cells and adds the CAR component which enhances their functions and kills cancer-specific receptors. The reason Immunotherapy is more successful than others is because it carries the least amount of side-effects. Another method used is chemotherapy, which is a double-edged sword. Not only does it wipe out the cancer cells, but it also harms the rest of our cells, making it impractical.

By Raymond Bui

THE GAP SEMESTER 01/2019 – 07/2019

Attend Blood Cancer Conference 1/26/19

Learn few terminology words and systemic Disease Cancer

- Multiple Myeloma is the cancer of plasma cells which
- found mainly in Bone Marrow.
- Lymphoma is a group of cancers that affected the lymphatic system. Hodgkin Lymphoma vs Non-Hodgkin Lymphoma.
- Autologous Stem cell Transplantation treatment is to use own stem cell to delay the progression of certain blood cancer.
- Allogeneic Stem cell Transplantation treatment is to use donor stem cell to restore patient's marrow and blood cells.
- Adoptive cell Therapy uses a patient's immune cells to fight cancer, cells expanded or enriched in an outside engineering process before being re-infused into patients. Engineered T cell that is equipped with special receptors that target specific proteins on cancer cells and eliminate those cells. This is new FDA-approved Treatment for Lymphoma and Leukemia.
- Key Notes Speaker, Dr Rick Klausner stated CAR-T cell Therapy is a new breakthrough for some blood cancer treatment. There is still challenge in applying CAR-T cell approach for solid tumors. But what had it been for the next decade to overcome the challenge.

BLOOD CANCER CONFERENCE

NORTHERN CALIFORNIA 2019

A Free Educational Conference for Patients, Survivors, Caregivers and Healthcare Professionals

This Blood Cancer Conference (BCC) is one of many programs developed by The Leukemia & Lymphoma Society (LLS) to meet the needs of patients, survivors, families and oncology professionals, the people who deal with blood cancer every day and the people who care for them. BCC attendees receive the most current information and access to local resources to help navigate and make informed decisions about their treatment and survivorship.

SATURDAY JANUARY 26, 2019
9:00AM – 2:00PM
HYATT REGENCY SAN FRANCISCO
5 Embarcadero Center
San Francisco, CA 94111

REGISTRATION INFORMATION
This is a free program for patients, survivors, families, caregivers and healthcare professionals* but **REGISTRATION IS REQUIRED**.

PHONE: 866.450.0669
ONLINE: www.etouches.com/ncabcc19
EMAIL: SF.BCC@LLS.org

For questions, please contact:
Thea Sigerman, Patient Access Manager
SF.BCC@lls.org | 866.450.0669

*This is NOT a continuing education (CE) program.

9:00 AM	Registration, Exhibits, Breakfast & Visiting in the Ballroom
10:00 AM	**Concurrent Morning Breakout Sessions**
	Multiple Myeloma — Thomas Martin, MD, UCSF Comprehensive Cancer Center
	Non-Hodgkin Lymphoma (NHL) – High Grade and Hodgkin Lymphoma — Chaitra Ujjani, MD, Seattle Cancer Care Alliance
	Chronic Lymphocytic Leukemia (CLL) — Tanya Siddiqi, MD, City of Hope
	Myeloproliferative Neoplasms (MPN) — Bart Scott, MD, Seattle Cancer Care Alliance
	Non-Hodgkin Lymphoma (NHL) – Low Grade — Babis Andreadis, MD, UCSF Comprehensive Cancer Center
	Chronic Myeloid Leukemia (CML) — Neil Shah, MD, PhD, UCSF Comprehensive Cancer Center
	Adult Acute Leukemias (AML & ALL) — Karin Gaensler, MD, UCSF Comprehensive Cancer Center
	Myelodysplastic Syndromes (MDS) — Brian Jonas, MD, PhD, UC Davis Cancer Center
	New Active Coping Strategies for Caregivers — Barbara Kivowitz, MSW, Author Love in the Time of Chronic Illness: How to Fight the Sickness, Not Each Other
11:20 AM	Break/Exhibitor Session
11:40 AM	**Lunch**
	This Is LLS — Lauren Hall, MSW, MPH, Sr. Director, Patient Access
	Survivorship Session: Managing Anxiety and Fear of Recurrence — Sheila Lahijani, MD, Stanford University Medical Center
1:00 PM	**Keynote**
	Curing Heme Malignancies with CAR T-Cells — Rick Klausner, MD, Founder and CEO Lyell Immunopharma, Founder and Director, GRAIL
2:00 PM	Evaluations and Conference Concludes

THANK YOU TO OUR NATIONAL SPONSORS

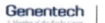 

We look forward to seeing you at the Northern California Blood Cancer Conference! We believe it is crucial to our mission to provide FREE education and information to all individuals diagnosed with a blood cancer and those who care for them. We appreciate your interest and look forward to seeing you on January 26, 2019. Please note that while this conference is free to attend, LLS and its sponsors pay for each participant to make the conference possible. Consequently, it is important to cancel your reservation right away if your plans change or you are unable to attend.

Princeton Review and MCAT

123 hours of live content class and Strategy Practice and Practice.

E.M.T. vs Hospital Volunteer

National Registry Emergency Medical Technicians

Hereby Certifies

Raymond Bui

as a

Emergency Medical Technician

duly registered together with all the rights and privileges appertaining thereto in consideration of having satisfied the prescribed national standards for certification. In Testimony Whereof, the seal of National Registry of Emergency Medical Technicians and the Signatures as authorized by the Board of Directors are hereunto affixed this Fourteenth day of July, 2018 A.D.

Chairman of Board   *Executive Director*

E.M.T PAID POSITION Vs JOB SHADOW IN HOSPITAL

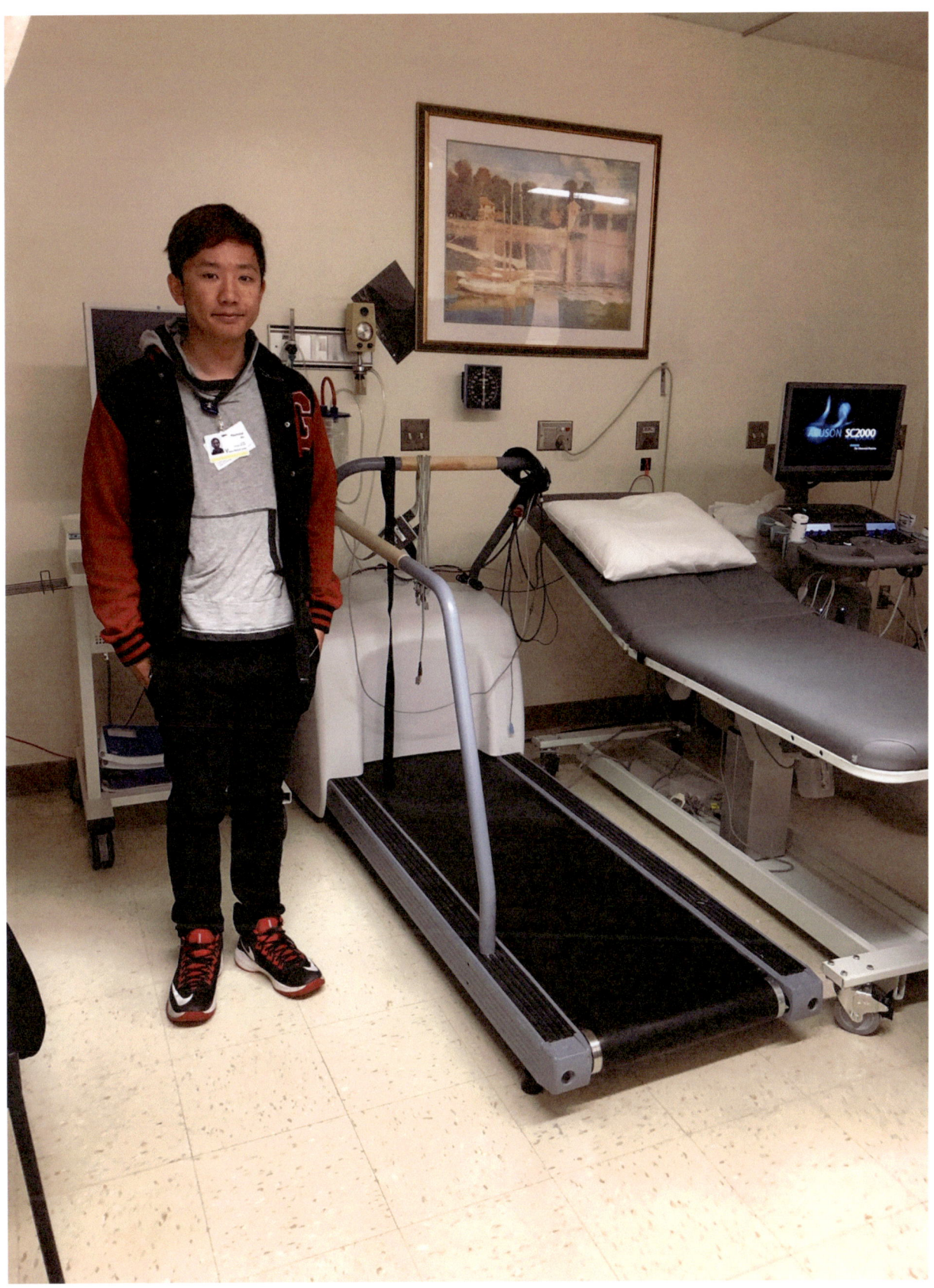

VASCULAR LAB

College Graduation May 18, 2019

Printed by Libri Plureos GmbH in Hamburg, Germany